CHRISTIAN FESTIVALS COOKBOOK

SAVIOUR PIROTTA
WITH PHOTOGRAPHY BY ZUL MUKHIDA

HODDER
Wayland

An imprint of Hodder Children's Books

D1631717

CLASS	BARCODE
641.566	R86187A

DATE - 6 DEC 2004

SOUTH KENT COLLEGE
ASHFORD LEARNING CENTRE

FESTIVALS COOKBOOKS

CHRISTIAN FESTIVALS COOKBOOK

HINDU FESTIVALS COOKBOOK

JEWISH FESTIVALS COOKBOOK

CHINESE FESTIVALS COOKBOOK

NB: Nuts are contained in some of the recipes in this book
(see pages 14–15, 16).
Nuts may provoke a dangerous allergic reaction in some people.

 © 2000 White-Thomson Publishing Ltd

Produced for Hodder Wayland by Margot Richardson
23 Hanover Terrace, Brighton, E Sussex, BN2 2SN, UK

Food photography: Zul Mukhida, Chapel Studios, Brighton
Designer: Tim Mayer
Illustrations: Tim Mayer
Proofreader: Philippa Smith

Published in Great Britain in 2000 by Hodder Wayland,
an imprint of Hodder Children's Books

The right of Saviour Pirotta to be identified as the author of this
Work has been asserted by him in accordance with the Copyright,
Designs and Patents Act 1988.

Picture acknowledgements:
Art Directors and TRIP 17 (J Isachsen), 19 (J Greenberg), 29 (H Rogers);
Axiom 4 (Conor Caffrey), 18 (Conor Caffrey), Eye Ubiquitous 6
(L Fordyce); Impact Photos 5 (Adrian Sherratt), 7 (Christophe Pluntzer).

All instructions, information and advice given in this book are
believed to be reliable and accurate. All guidelines and warnings
should be read carefully and the author, packager, editor and
publisher cannot accept responsibility for injuries or damage
arising out of failure to comply with the same.

All rights reserved. No part of this publication may be reproduced,
stored in a retrieval system, or transmitted, in any form or by any
means without the prior written permission of the publisher, nor be
otherwise circulated in any form of binding or cover other than that
in which it is published and without a similar condition being
imposed on the subsequent purchaser.

A catalogue record for this book is available from the British Library.

ISBN 0 7502 2633 1

Printed and bound by G. Canale & C.S.p.A., Turin

Hodder Children's Books
A division of Hodder Headline
338 Euston Road, London NW1 3BH

CONTENTS

CHRISTIAN FESTIVALS AND FOOD

Christians believe that there is one God, who made the world and all its people. Soon after the first man and woman had been created, they disobeyed God and He was not pleased with them any more. The gates to heaven were shut. Then, after a great many years, God sent his son, Jesus Christ, to save the world.

Jesus came into the world as a baby. As He grew up, He brought teachings from God to show people how to live good lives. But some people did not like what He said, and eventually had Him killed on a cross.

However, three days later Jesus rose from the dead. This made it possible for people to enter heaven. In fact, Christians think that anyone who believes in God will not disappear when they die, but have 'everlasting life'.

Pictures or scenes telling the story of the birth of Jesus are often displayed at Christmas. These statues show the infant Jesus and his parents, Joseph and Mary.

Easter celebrations in Guatemala, South America. The holy figures have been carried from the church for an outdoor parade.

Since then, Christians have celebrated both the day when Jesus was born, Christmas, and the day He rose from the dead, Easter. These are the two main festivals in the Christian year.

SaFety anD HyGiene

When cutting with knives, frying, boiling and using the oven, ALWAYS ask an adult to help you.

Food must always be kept clean. Food that gets dirty will not taste good – and can even make people sick.

Always wash your hands before you start cooking.

Do not wipe dirty hands on a towel. Wash your hands first.

If you need to taste something while cooking, use a clean fork or spoon.

Make sure work surfaces are clean and dry. This includes tables, worktops and chopping boards.

Christians who are very devout prepare themselves for both festivals with long periods of prayer, thinking and fasting. But the festivals themselves are celebrated with joyous services, family gatherings and, of course, lots of delicious food.

This book shows you how to prepare some of these festive foods. The recipes have been collected from around the world. They range from simple savoury dishes to fancy cakes and sweet treats.

Easter

Easter Sunday marks the day when Jesus rose from the dead and made it possible for people to enter heaven. For many Christians, it is the most holy and joyous day of the year.

Holy Week starts on Palm Sunday, a week before Easter Sunday. Palm Sunday marks the day when Jesus entered the city of Jerusalem. He had come to celebrate the Jewish feast of Passover, and, as He arrived, many people came out to greet Him, waving the branches of palm trees.

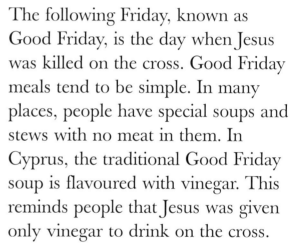

The following Friday, known as Good Friday, is the day when Jesus was killed on the cross. Good Friday meals tend to be simple. In many places, people have special soups and stews with no meat in them. In Cyprus, the traditional Good Friday soup is flavoured with vinegar. This reminds people that Jesus was given only vinegar to drink on the cross.

Easter Sunday is the climax of Holy Week. Traditional Easter meals are full of rich foods, such as meat and cream. There are luxurious Easter cakes too, as well as biscuits, puddings, sweet breads and, of course, Easter eggs.

This procession in the Philippines acts out the story of Good Friday, when Jesus wore a crown of thorns and was forced to carry a cross by Roman soldiers.

The early Christian leaders liked celebrating Easter in spring, when the Earth is being re-born after the long, cold winter. Many other people held spring festivals at this time of the year, including the ancient Greeks, Persians and Romans. They gave each other eggs, the symbol of new life.

Christians adopted eggs as the symbol of Easter, painting them in bright colours and patterns to reflect the happiness of spring and of Jesus rising from the dead. Today, real painted eggs or chocolate ones are given as Easter presents.

In Greece, a special bread is made for Easter Sunday. In this parade through the streets, a picture of Jesus is carried in front of the bread.

7

Hot Cross Buns

Preparation time: 2¹/₂ hours

Cooking time: 20 minutes

Oven temperature: 190 °C/ Gas Mark 5

Makes: 15–20 buns

Ingredients

1 tbsp dried yeast

150 ml warm water

50 ml milk

50 g margarine

30 g sugar

¹/₂ tsp salt

1 tsp mixed spice

450 g plain white flour

2 eggs

25 g raisins

25 g mixed peel

Equipment

2 large mixing bowls

Wooden spoon

Small saucepan

Clingfilm

Baking tray

Knife

Clean tea-towel

During Lent, and especially on Good Friday, many people eat hot cross buns. These are small bread buns decorated with a cross on top. It is said that this cross is a symbol of Jesus saving the world. Hot cross buns are especially popular in the UK and the USA. Serve the buns while still warm with a little butter for spreading.

1 Put the yeast in a large bowl. Add the warm water and the milk. Stir gently until the yeast is dissolved.

2 Ask an adult to melt the margarine in a saucepan and add it to the yeast. Also add the sugar, salt, spice and half the flour. Beat gently until smooth.

3 Beat in the eggs one at a time. Then add the mixed peel, the raisins and the rest of the flour.

4 Sprinkle flour over the work surface. Turn out the mixture and knead with both hands until you have a dough. Add more flour if necessary.

5 Grease the other bowl with butter. Put the mixture into the bowl, cover it with clingfilm and leave it to rise in a warm place. This should take about an hour.

6 Divide the dough into 15–20 pieces and carefully roll them into balls. Don't press them too hard or they will not rise very well.

7 Put the buns on a greased baking tray. Cut the shape of a cross on the top of each bun. Cover the buns with a clean tea-towel and let them rise again until they have doubled in size. Ask an adult to pre-heat the oven. Bake the buns for about 20 minutes. Let them cool a little before serving.

Greek Roast Lamb

Preparation time: 1 day

Cooking time: 2–2½ hours

Oven temperature:
180 °C/Gas Mark 4

Serves: 8

Ingredients

2 cloves of garlic

2 lemons

1 tbsp dried or fresh rosemary

3 tbsp olive oil

1.5 kg leg of lamb

20 small potatoes

Salt and pepper

Sprigs of fresh rosemary

Equipment

Chopping knife

Lemon squeezer

Small bowl

Tablespoons

Large dish with high sides to hold lamb

Roasting tin

Potato peeler

The lamb is the symbol of Jesus dying to save the world. The early Christians ate lamb meat to mark His gift to them. In the ninth century, the Pope made roast lamb his official Easter dinner. It is still the traditional Easter meal in many Christian homes.

Serve on a platter garnished with fresh rosemary.

1 Make a marinade. Ask an adult to help you chop the garlic finely. Squeeze the lemons. Mix together the garlic, lemon juice, rosemary, and 1 tbsp of the olive oil.

2 Ask an adult to score the lamb with a sharp knife, so that it is covered in cuts that are about 2 cm deep.

3 Place the lamb in a dish and pour the marinade over it. Put it in the fridge and leave overnight. Turn it over, and spoon the juices over it regularly.

4 Put the lamb in a roasting tin. Season with salt and pepper. Then pour the marinade over it. Add the other 2 tbsp of olive oil.

5 Peel the potatoes. Put the potatoes around the lamb in the tin.

6 Ask an adult to bake it in the oven for 2–2½ hours. Spoon the juices over often. (Add some water if the potatoes get too dry.)

Colomba

This special Easter bread comes from Italy. Colomba means dove in Italian. The dove is a symbol of peace.

People bake special Easter cakes, pastries and fancy breads in many countries around the world. Most of these recipes use yeast, which makes the dough rise. This reminds people of Jesus rising from the dead. This recipe does not use yeast, but makes a light, crumbly bread.

Preparation time: 45 minutes

Cooking time: 10 minutes

Oven temperature: 230 °C/ Gas Mark 8

Makes: 1 large dove

Ingredients

225 g self-raising flour

1/2 level tsp salt

1 level tsp baking powder

2 level tbsp caster sugar

60 g soft margarine

1 orange

60 g mixed dried fruit

150 ml milk

60 g blanched almonds

Icing sugar, for dusting

Equipment

Large mixing bowl

Grater

Wooden spoon

Baking tray

Non-stick baking parchment

Wire rack

Sieve

1 Put the flour, salt, baking powder and sugar into the mixing bowl.

2 Add the margarine in small pieces and rub it into the flour with your hands, until it looks like breadcrumbs.

3 Use the fine part of the grater to remove the orange's skin (called 'zest').

4 Add the orange zest, dried fruit and milk. Stir to form a soft dough.

5 Turn out on to a floured surface and knead very lightly with your hands. Form into two flat torpedo shapes, one slightly smaller than the other.

6 Line the baking tray with baking parchment and place the large shape on it. Put the other shape on top, diagonally, to form the dove's wings.

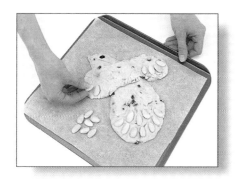

7 Decorate the wings with almonds, to look like feathers, and use raisins for eyes.

8 Ask an adult to pre-heat the oven. Bake for about 10 minutes, or until golden brown. Cool on a wire rack. Dust with icing sugar, using the sieve.

Figolla

Preparation / decorating time: 1 hour

Cooking time: 20 minutes

Oven temperature: 180 °C/ Gas Mark 4

Makes: 3–4 figollas

Ingredients

500 g packet ready-made sweet pastry

450 g marzipan

Icing sugar

Food colouring for icing

Coloured foil, sprinkles, silver balls, tubes of writing icing, etc

Small chocolate Easter egg in foil

Equipment

Rolling pin

Fish templates

Knife

Spatula

Baking tray

Medium mixing bowls

Spoons

Wire rack

Here is a special Easter-egg pastry from Malta. You can make it in the shape of a lamb, rabbit, child, basket or a fish – an early Christian symbol. Draw the shape first on a piece of cardboard and cut it out to make a template. It should be about 10 cm long. Then make a second template from the first, about 1 cm smaller all round.

Make your figolla as colourful as you wish. Then wrap it in cellophane and tie with a coloured ribbon.

1 Roll out the pastry with a rolling pin so that it is 5 mm thick. Using the fish template, cut out two fish shapes from the pastry.

2 Roll out the marzipan so that it is about 5 mm thick. Using the second, smaller template, cut out a smaller fish shape from the marzipan.

3 Put the marzipan shape on top of a pastry shape. Put the second pastry shape on top and seal the edges with your finger dipped in a little bit of water. Ask an adult to pre-heat the oven.

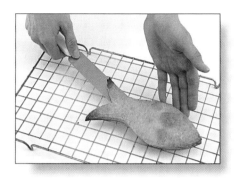

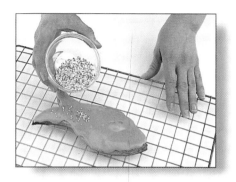

4 Using the spatula, place the fish on a baking tray. Ask an adult to bake in the oven for 15–20 minutes or until golden brown. Cool on a wire rack.

5 To make icing, mix a few spoonfuls of icing sugar with a little hot water. Add a few drops of food colouring.

6 Cover the figolla with icing. Before it sets, decorate it with coloured foil, sprinkles or silver balls.

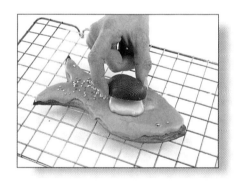

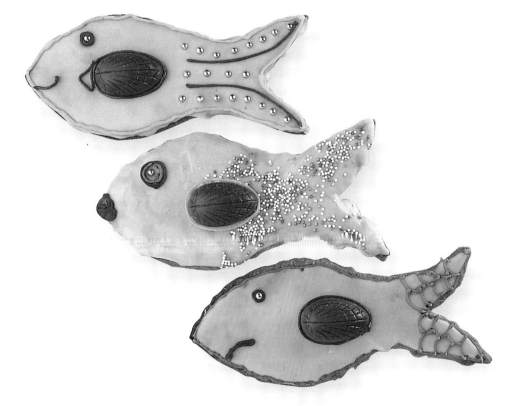

7 Divide an Easter egg in two. Put a blob of icing in the centre of the figolla. Put the egg in the blob and let it set. Finish the decoration with icing.

Cassata Ice-cream

Cassata is a popular Italian dessert often eaten at Easter. In the past, when people were forbidden to use eggs and milk products during Lent, before Easter, everyone looked forward to an Easter treat with milk or cheese in it. Today, most people do not give up dairy products for Lent but these foods are still popular.

Preparation time: 1 hour

Freezing time: 2 hours

Serves: 10

Ingredients

2 litres vanilla ice-cream

1 litre strawberry ice-cream

Green food colouring

50 g pistachio nuts, crushed

50 g mixed candied fruit

Equipment

Large loaf tin

Clingfilm

Mixing bowls

Spoons

Rubber spatula

Knife

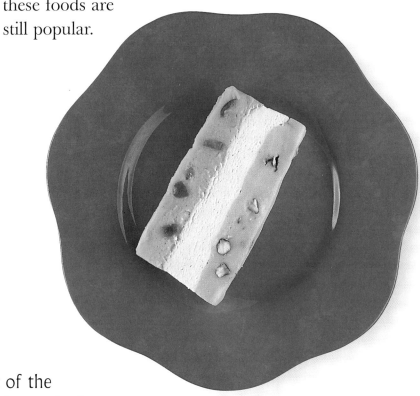

1 Take the vanilla ice-cream out of the freezer and let it soften a bit. Line a loaf tin with clingfilm.

2 Put half the vanilla ice-cream into a bowl. Add a drop of green food colouring and mix with a spoon until all the ice-cream is green. Mix in the crushed pistachio nuts.

3 Pour the green ice-cream into the tin and pat down to form a smooth layer. Return to the freezer and allow to harden.

4 Take other half of the vanilla ice-cream. Make a white layer on top of the green one. Put the tin back in the freezer again.

5 Soften the strawberry ice cream. Mix in the candied fruit. Make a third layer in the loaf tin and re-freeze.

6 When you want to serve, use the clingfilm to help pull the Cassata out of the tin. Cut into slices with a knife.

OTHER EASTER FOODS

Easter breads, buns and cakes vary from one country to another. Slovak Easter bread is decorated with bits of pastry moulded in the shapes of birds. The Italians make *Tortona*, a piece of dough twisted round an egg.

Bread decorated with whole, cooked eggs can also be found in Bulgaria. In the past, the egg shells were painted bright red to remind people of the blood of Jesus when he died. Today, other colours are used too. The bread is taken to church to be blessed by a priest. As the people leave the church after the service, they crack one of the eggs against the wall. It is the first egg they have eaten for weeks.

Eggs are also dyed or painted in other countries, such as Austria, Romania, the Ukraine and Sweden. In France, some children spend Easter morning hunting for hidden chocolate eggs.

In the Azores, people eat a special omelette called *Omeleta Pascal*. It is made with eggs laid on Good Friday and served with pieces of bacon or sausage.

In African countries, Easter dinner might be chicken with roasted or boiled rice.

Decorated Easter eggs are still made and sold in Austria. This market is in Vienna.

CHRISTMAS

People used to hold mid-winter festivals long before Jesus was born. In ancient times many people were scared that the sun would not return to their country after winter. The Scandinavians would send a search party to look for it. When the travellers returned with news that they had seen the great sun returning, a festival would be held. It was called Yuletide. People gathered around a burning Yule log and had a great feast.

The Romans had perhaps the most lavish of mid-winter festivals. It was called the Saturnalia, and it was held in honour of their god, Saturn. The festival started on 17th December and lasted for seven days. Roman people exchanged gifts, held great banquets and decorated their houses with greenery. They even decked green trees with burning candles, like the lights on present-day Christmas trees.

In some countries, Santa Claus is believed to visit children on Christmas Eve, bringing presents in a sleigh pulled by reindeer. Although the story comes from Europe, this photograph was taken in Mexico City.

The early Christians were, of course, forbidden to worship false gods. So they adapted the Saturnalia festival to fit their new faith. Instead of worshipping Saturn, they celebrated the birth of Jesus. No one really knew what time of the year Jesus was born, so the church leaders decided that mid-winter was just as good as any time to remember his birthday. In AD 350, the Pope decreed that Christmas should be celebrated on 25th December. It's been like that ever since.

In the past, many people used up the last of their fresh food during the winter festivals. They also made cakes and puddings with foods that kept through the long winter months, such as dried fruit, nuts, flour and spices. As Christianity spread around the world, these treats were adapted for Christmas. Many are still popular to this very day.

A lavish gingerbread house made in Florida, USA.

West African Couscous

Preparation time: 15 minutes

Cooking time: 1 hour

Serves: 8

Ingredients

2 small onions

3 carrots

3 courgettes

1 cup raisins

8 tbsp (½ cup) vegetable oil

2 kg chicken, cut into large pieces

1 chicken stock cube

1 tsp turmeric

1 tsp cumin

1 tsp mixed spice

½ tsp salt

410 g tin cooked chickpeas

450 g dried couscous

2 tbsp butter

Equipment

Cutting knife

Large saucepan

Wooden spoons

Tin opener

Bowl or pan for cooking couscous

Fork

Large plate

Ladle

Every country has its favourite Christmas dinner. The British, French and Americans prefer roast turkey. This couscous is not only a favourite dish in Africa, it is also eaten by people of African origin everywhere. In the USA it is served during the Kwanzaa celebrations, when African-Americans thank the earth for all its bounty.

1 Ask an adult to help you chop the onions, carrots and courgettes. Soak the raisins in warm water.

2 With an adult's help, heat the oil in the saucepan and soften the onions. Add the chicken and fry until golden brown.

3 Turn down the heat. Add the stock cube, spices and salt. Stir well. Pour in 600 ml water. Cook gently for half an hour.

4 Add the vegetables to the saucepan. Cook on a gentle heat until they are cooked but still a bit crunchy.

5 Add the chickpeas. Keep the stew warm over a very low heat.

6 Cook the couscous, following the instructions on the packet. Drain the raisins. Mix them and the butter into the couscous, fluffing it up with a fork.

7 Turn out the couscous on to a large plate. Very gently, form it into a mound. Ladle the chicken and the vegetables around the couscous. Serve with the sauce from the stew.

Tamales

Preparation time: 1½ hours

Cooking time: 1½ hours

Oven temperature: 180 °C/ Gas Mark 4

Makes: 10 tamales

Ingredients

3 small onions

1 clove garlic

3 tbsp vegetable oil

900 g ground beef

2 tbsp tomato paste

Pinch cayenne pepper

Pinch salt

1 beef stock cube

180 g cornmeal

Equipment

Sharp knife

Garlic crusher

Frying pan

Wooden spoons

Saucepan

Spoon

10 x 20 cm squares kitchen foil

Baking dish

These Mexican beef patties (pronounced 'tam-<u>arl</u>-ays') are also popular in Costa Rica. Some people give them as presents, while others have them as a special treat after midnight mass on Christmas Eve, or for Christmas dinner.

In the past, these delicious packages of cornmeal and meat were wrapped in the green husks of corn cobs. Foil is used here, though, as it is easier to find and to use.

Serve the tamales hot with tomato sauce.

1 With an adult's help, chop the onions finely and crush the garlic.

2 Ask an adult to help you heat the oil in the frying pan and soften the onions. Add the beef and the garlic and fry until brown.

3 Add the tomato paste, the cayenne pepper, salt and crumbled stock cube. Cook on a very low flame for an hour.

4 While the meat is cooking, put 1 litre of water in the saucepan. Ask an adult to bring to the boil and add the cornmeal. Turn down the heat.

5 An adult should stir until the mixture thickens. Turn the heat right down and simmer for about 30 minutes. Then let the cornmeal cool down.

6 Spread 1 spoonful of cornmeal on each square of foil and top that with 2 spoonfuls of beef. Carefully roll up the foil parcels. Pre-heat the oven.

7 Put the parcels in the baking dish. Pour over about 200 ml water. Cook in the oven for $1\frac{1}{2}$ hours.

Gingerbread House

Preparation/decorating time: 1½ hours

Cooking time: 10 minutes

Oven temperature: 180 °C/ Gas Mark 4

Makes: 1 large house shape

Ingredients

6 tbsp golden syrup

2 tbsp black treacle

90 g brown sugar

90 g butter

450 g self-raising flour

1 tbsp ground ginger

Pinch bicarbonate of soda

2 egg yolks

Tubes of ready-made writing icing

Sweets and shapes for decorating

Equipment

Small saucepan

Wooden spoons

Large mixing bowl

Rolling pin

Non-stick baking parchment

Knife

Baking tray

Wire rack

Gingerbread houses come from Germany, where ginger is associated with the town of Nürnberg. They look a little like dolls' houses with four walls, sloping roofs, doors and windows, all decorated with icing and sweets. Here is a flat house shape to make. Have fun decorating it.

1 In a saucepan, put the syrup, treacle, sugar and butter. Ask an adult to stir and mix over a low heat until they melt and combine.

2 Put the flour, ground ginger and the bicarbonate of soda in a large mixing bowl. Add the egg yolks and mix slowly.

3 With an adult's help, add the syrup mixture and stir with a wooden spoon to form a dough.

4 Turn out on to a floured surface and knead until smooth.

5 Roll out the dough on top of baking parchment paper. Make it about 1.5 cm thick. With a knife, cut out the shape of a house. Pre-heat the oven.

6 Grease a baking tray. Use the baking parchment to lift the shape and place it on the tray. Cook in a moderate oven until golden brown: about 10 minutes.

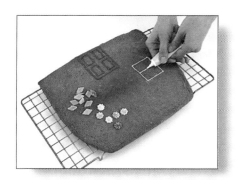

7 Let the gingerbread cool on a wire rack. Then draw in the doors and windows with coloured icing. Decorate with sweets, stuck on with more icing.

Roscón de Reyes

Preparation / decorating
time: 45 minutes

Cooking time: 1 hour

Oven temperature:
180 °C / Gas Mark 4

Serves: 12

Ingredients

150 g margarine

300 g self-raising flour

150 g caster sugar

2 eggs

200 ml milk

1 large dried bean (wrapped
in kitchen foil)

Strawberry jam

1 can 'spray' whipped cream

Equipment

1.7 litre ring cake tin

Large mixing bowl

Small saucepan

Wooden spoon

Wire rack

Sharp knife

Spoon

The name of this cake means 'crown of the kings' (and is pronounced 'ros-kon day rayas'). In Spain, the day of the three kings is a bigger celebration than Christmas itself. Called Epiphany, it is celebrated on 6th January and marks the end of the holiday season. In most towns and villages, there are parades with three men dressed as kings (*reyes*).

This 'crown' cake is based on a traditional Spanish version. It has a bean hidden inside it. Whoever finds the 'prize' can look forward to a year brimming with good luck.

1 Grease the ring tin with a little margarine. Ask an adult to pre-heat the oven.

2 Put the flour and the sugar into a large mixing bowl.

3 Put the margarine in a small saucepan, over a low heat. When it has melted, stir it into the flour and sugar.

4 Add the milk, a little at a time, and beat the mixture again.

5 Beat the eggs, one at a time, into the cake mixture.

6 Pour the mixture into the ring tin. Insert the bean, wrapped in foil. Bake for about 50 minutes, or until cooked.

7 Cool the cake on a wire rack. Cut it in half and fill it with strawberry jam and whipped cream. Cut into slices and serve.

Pepparkakor

These Swedish biscuits are the perfect Christmas treat. People make them to give as gifts, or to share with friends who drop by with Christmas greetings. Others can be hung on a Christmas tree as decorations.

Preparation/decorating time: 2 hours (over 2 days)

Cooking time: 10 minutes

Oven temperature: 180 °C/Gas Mark 4

Makes: 30 biscuits (approx)

Ingredients

100 g golden syrup

100 g butter, softened

100 g sugar

300 g self-raising flour

1/2 tsp ground ginger

1/2 tsp ground cinnamon

1 egg, beaten

Tubes of ready-made writing icing

Equipment

Large saucepan

Wooden spoon

Large mixing bowl

Clingfilm

Rolling pin

Cookie cutters

Baking tray

Egg slice

Wire rack

1 Put the syrup into a large saucepan. Ask an adult to heat it until it is boiling. Then turn the heat down and let it bubble for 2 more minutes.

2 With an adult's help, add the butter and the sugar. Mix with a wooden spoon until the butter has melted. Take off the heat and allow to cool slightly but not to harden.

3 Mix together the flour, ginger, cinnamon and salt in a large bowl. Add the syrup mixture and the egg, and mix into a dough.

4 Cover the bowl with clingfilm and keep it overnight in the fridge.

5 Roll out dough into wafer-thin pieces. Use cookie cutters in the shape of hearts, stars, Christmas trees and animals. For Christmas-tree decorations, make a hole at the top of each biscuit.

6 Put on a baking tray and bake in a moderate oven for 5–8 minutes or until a light, golden brown. Cool on a wire rack.

7 Decorate with writing icing, then store in airtight containers until needed.

OTHER CHRISTMAS FOODS

All over the world, people eat a lavish Christmas dinner, but the details vary not only from one country to another but also from region to region. In the UK, the USA and Australasia, the main Christmas meal is eaten on Christmas Day. Other people, including those in Austria, Denmark, Germany and Poland, prefer to have their celebration dinner on Christmas Eve (the night before Christmas).

In the Provence region of France, people fast the day before Christmas. But after midnight mass they tuck into a giant feast called *le gros souper*. The many courses might include snails with garlic, dried cod and braised celery. In the past, these were followed by no less than thirteen puddings. Today, however, most people can only manage one or two puddings.

A Greek family enjoys a traditional Christmas dinner of roast meat and vegetables.

In Poland, Christmas dinner is called the *Wigilia* and has twelve courses. Each course represents one of the twelve apostles. The meal starts when the evening star, symbolizing the star of Bethlehem, appears in the night sky. No meat is served but one of the courses might be fish, such as carp, pike or herring. Before the meal, thin wafers called *oplatki* are broken into pieces and shared between family members. They are stamped with scenes of Christmas and have been blessed by the priest in church.

Christianitiy is perhaps an unusual religion in that it has only a few festivals, and only Easter and Christmas are celebrated with any specific foods. Harvest Festival involves food, obviously, but usually in an unprepared state, representing the products of farming. Thanksgiving in the USA is always marked by a family meal of roast turkey with cranberry sauce, but, with the passing of time, it has little religious significance for most Americans.

> When using the recipes contained in this book, children should be supervised by one or more adults at all times. This especially applies when cutting with knives, cooking on a cooker hob and using the oven.

EQUIPMENT

The recipes are written on the understanding that adults have access to weighing and measuring equipment such as scales and measuring jugs. These are not mentioned specifically in the instructions.

Non-stick baking parchment: this is specified for some of the recipes that involve baking in the oven. It is extremely effective for preventing cakes and biscuits from sticking to metal trays. It is also a very handy aid for moving large shapes from work surface to baking tray. However, if you cannot buy it, used well-oiled greaseproof paper instead.

COOKING METHODS

Hot cross buns: In an effort to keep this recipe as simple as possible, the crosses are made by scoring the dough prior to baking. The crosses can be made more prominent by laying thin strips of pastry along these cuts.

Figolla: Make sure that the pastry shapes are properly sealed around the marzipan filling, or the filling will leak out during baking. After baking, the pastry shape can break fairly easily, so take care during the decorating process to avoid accidents.

Tamales: Teachers or parents may wish to prepare the cornmeal in advance and have children cook just the meat and assemble the packages. If the cornmeal is cooked by children, take care to keep it on a low heat: if it boils too rapidly it can spit unpleasantly, and it will also stick easily to the bottom of the pan.

Gingerbread house: Adults can help children to make a three-dimensional house.

You will need two large rectangles for the roof, two small rectangles for the house's front and back, and two sides that are rectangular at the bottom and slope to a point at the top. Make cardboard templates first and check that they are the correct shape. Then make the shapes from gingerbread.

To assemble the house, place the sides upright on a cake board with the edges touching, keeping them in place with heavy food tins. Using thick icing, stick the pieces to the cake board and to each other. Spread some icing along the top edges of the house and stick on the roof panels. Use thick, rough white icing to cover the roof with 'snow'.

Roscón de Reyes: This is traditionally made with a sweet yeast dough. The finished cakes are sometimes decorated with a cardboard crown, worn by the lucky winner of the bean inside.

Topic Web

Glossary

Apostles The twelve men who were followers of Jesus while he was on earth.

Decreed Ordered by someone who is very important, such as a king or the Pope.

Devout Having deep religious feelings or beliefs.

Dough Uncooked bread or pastry.

Fasting To stop eating some or all foods.

Heaven The place where God is believed to be, and where people who believe in Him go after they die.

Holy Devoted to God.

Hygienc Cleanliness.

Lent The period of about eight weeks before Easter.

Marinade A mixture of liquids, herbs and spices, put on food to make it tastier.

Mass A Christian ceremony in a church.

Persians People from the ancient country of Persia, a country now called Iran.

Pope The elected leader of the Catholic Church

Prayer Talking to God, by asking things, or saying thank you.

Procession A group of people moving togther.

Romans People who were citizens of the ancient

Roman empire. Also describes people who live, or were born, in Rome.

Savoury Food that is not sweet.

Scandinavians People from Scandinavian countries, including Denmark, Norway and Sweden.

Symbol A thing that gives an idea of something else. A symbol can be a mark, a sign or a picture.

Template A shape used to mark and cut out a number of the same shapes.

Worship Show love for God.

Yeast An ingredient that creates air bubbles in dough and makes it grow bigger.

INDEX

Page numbers in **bold** refer to photographs

RESOURCES

Books

Celebrate: Christmas by Mike Hirst (Hodder Wayland, 1999)

Christmas Carols by by H. Amery (Usborne Publishing, 1998)

Christian Festival Tales by Saviour Pirotta, illustrated by Helen Cann (Hodder Wayland, 2000)

Joy to the World by Saviour Pirotta, illustrated by Sheila Moxley (Frances Lincoln, 1998)

The Story of Easter by Aileen Fisher, illlustrated by Stefano Vitale (HarperCollins, 1998)

Web sites

http://www.holidays.net/christmas/index.htm. Christmas on the net. A fantastic site, part of the bigger 'Holiday on the Net' site, with stories, seasonal recipes and ideas for activities and decorations.

http://www.holidays.net/easter/index.htm Easter on the Net. A site with lots of information about Easter, games and activities. Learn all about Easter eggs and bunnies, and send your friends a holiday message.